RED ZONE FATHERING

48 PLAYS GREAT FATHERS MAKE

PATRICK DONOHUE

D1317887

DEDICATION

To my parents, Jim & Judy Donohue, who created a home where their children could thrive and follow their dreams.

To Vino & Devi Mankad, my in-laws, whose welcoming spirit made me feel part of the family from the first day we met.

To Binita, Shaan and Sarina Donohue, you guys are the ones who bring me hope, inspiration and joy everyday.

PRAISE FOR PAT DONOHUE'S

Red Zone Fathering:
48 Plays Great Fathers Make

"Just last night used Play #12 – [Wo]Man in Motion – *to its usual good effect. No, I'm not a dad, but I've seen Coach Pat in action and I can tell you two true things: he's the real deal and his smart book can help you parent like you want to."*
– Alice Cottingham, Consultant to foundations and community nonprofits

"Anyone who knows Pat and his family on a personal level will know that he is the perfect man, father and coach to author a book like this. As a father of 2 young children myself, I can't wait to apply what he is sharing in the pages and chapters of 48 Plays.*"*
– Andre Blom, Director of Rehabilitation, Illinois Bone & Joint

"I can't think of a more important "game on the line" than that of being a father, and Pat is the one you will want to turn to for insight and the 48 plays in the game plan for success as a father and in life."
– Dan Hughes, Co-Founder Broadlook Software, Division I football player

"Coach Pat is the quintessential coach and leader. He inspires people to be the best that they can be in sports and in life."
– Thomas Keegan, Founding Partner, Keegan Law

"Insightful and practical . . . a combination of educator and coach influence the suggestions proffered by 'Coach Pat.' While this is a book on fathering, I believe moms can learn a thing or two from it as well! A 'must read' for anyone who wants to 'win' at parenting.""
– Maria Ward, Career Educator

"Patrick Donohue through Red Zone Fathering *creates a clever and easy to understand playbook to help fathers raise children to both win in and love their lives."*
– D. Luke Iorio, CEO IPEC Coaching

"Seldom do any of us need a 180 degree change of direction. Often, we just need a nudge in the right direction. Pat does an accomplished job nudging us 48 times; 48 times that can be applied in almost infinite ways."
– Ian Carroll, Senior Pastor, Greater Chicago Church

ACKNOWLEDGEMENTS

The late Sherman Egan who showed me the impact a great father could have generationally.

Victor Kore, my creative designer, for your ideas and inspiration.

Alison Hamm, my editor, for your sharp eye and constructive comments.

Stan Webber, from the Coaches Office, for designing my plays with your awesome coaching software.

For those who have professionally mentored me: Jackie DeFazio, Noree Mares, Maria Ward, Bob McBride, Jim Schmid, Pete McGivern, Hugh Egan, Dave Frederick, Ian Carroll, and Frank Maggio, I appreciate you and the wisdom you have given me.

For great coaches who inspired me into a life of coaching: Bruce Barron, Jim Luther, Phil Finanger, Ron King, Stav Canakes, Bob Savre and Ron Wellman.

For my teammates from Edina, MN Rob Wassenaar, Tim Healy, Jim Williams, Mike Seasly and Steve Shaffter who taught me the value of loyalty, dedication and friendship.

Anita Ball, my daily teammate, who patiently puts up with my thousands of new ideas and quietly inspires.

Tom Keegan, Perry Marshall and Dan Mack for consistent friendship, challenge and encouragement.

For my mom Judy Donohue, the backbone of our family and my dad James Donohue, my first and greatest coach.

Mawi Asgedom, accomplished author and a man of inspiration and purpose who pushed me to finish this book and whom I am proud to call a friend.

Binita Donohue, my partner for over twenty-five years who embodies love, intelligence, compassion and challenge to be a great mother and wife. I would not be the person I am today without you.

TABLE OF CONTENTS

END OF 3RD QUARTER – SIDELINE REPORTER / 99

4TH QUARTER – UNIQUE FORMATIONS, PERSONAL DOMINANCE & TRICK PLAYS / 103

END OF GAME INTERVIEW / 129

POST-GAME INFORMATION / 133

FOREWORD

If you want to evoke deep emotion, just ask people to tell you about their father. Some will tell you devastating stories of how they survived without a father; others of how they survived with one. Still others will tell you inspiring stories of fathers who encouraged, who sacrificed, and had profound, lifelong impact.

Of course, it's easy as fathers to forget the impact we have, as we try to survive the business of everyday life. And that's why this book matters.

This book will help you unlock a simple truth. *If you are a father, you are a coach. And the game you coach with your kids is far more important than any Super Bowl or World Series.*

You make plays every day. And sometimes, it feels likes you are getting blitzed, down after down, like your team is riddled with injuries and you are flat out of time.

In the coming pages, Coach Pat will show you 48 critical "red zone" situations you will face as a father. These red zone scenarios will help you raise kids of both genders and all ages, from early childhood to college.

I like to call Pat the "Coach's Coach." I've spent the last thirteen years working with over 1,000,000 students and I've not met anyone with his depth of coaching strategies for teens and parents.

You absolutely will be a better father after reading this book.

Of course, your infant may still pee in your eye as mine did. And your teenager may still steal your car (mine hasn't yet). But if you read this book, you will see the blitzes before they come and have a winning playbook in hand.

Selamawi "Mawi" Asgedom
President, Mawi Learning

KICK-OFF

It was a clear Friday night in September of 1982, the fourth game of my senior year football season for the Edina Hornets (in Minnesota). I was perched 15 yards deep in my free safety spot when I saw a wobbly pass sailing my way. Could it be this easy? An interception under the lights in front of thousands of screaming fans? Unbelievable, I thought. But yes, it was that easy. I picked off the first pass of my varsity career. As I trotted off the field to the low-fives of my teammates, I thought, There is nothing better than playing football, Friday night under the lights.

I wrote this book because I am passionate about both the game of football and the importance of fathering. Even though I also played baseball and basketball in high school, nothing beat the feeling of running out on the football field on a Friday night. I absolutely loved the camaraderie of being on the team and the sense of purpose and mission we had each week.

I think great fathers attack their role with the same sense of mission and purpose we had on the football field. I have been an educator and coach for over 20 years and one thing is totally clear to me: Fathers really matter. In all my years in schools, I've found one axiom that is consistently true—most well-adjusted and happy kids have a positive relationship with their father or a father substitute person. Most disturbed and unmotivated kids have a negative or nonexistent relationship with their fathers. Numerous research studies would tell us that the father's relationship to his children is a crucial factor in them developing a strong sense of identity. There is something special and profound about a father saying, "I think you can do this" or, "I believe in you."

Fathering, like the game of football, is not for the faint of heart. Both endeavors require skill, strategy and courage. Especially courage. A great father is a combination of a leader, counselor, coach, drill sergeant and cheerleader. Knowing how and when to play each role is the key to becoming a great father.

My hope is that the plays in this book will provide fathers with information and inspiration to be great. Fathering, like football, is about calling the right play at the right time and executing it. This playbook is filled with real-life scenarios that fathers face every day. Each play will provide suggestions on how to be great and how to avoid penalty flags, along with a little bit of football knowledge.

All great football teams are able to execute a variety of plays in multiple situations. There are offensive plays, defensives plays and special teams plays that all contribute to a winning game plan. Fathering is no different. We need to be able to execute on a variety of plays. This playbook provides all three types of plays—offensive, defensive, and special teams.

For most men, success in a career is a paramount goal. I am all for career success, but it pales in comparison to the importance of being a great father. Great fathers not only impact their own children; their influence rings down through generations.

At the 1992 Summer Olympic Games in Barcelona, Derek Redmond tore his hamstring midway through the 400-meter race in the semi-finals. After he hobbled a few feet, clearly in excruciating pain, his father, Jim, rushed to the track, fighting his way past race officials to get to his son. As the crowd looked on, Jim put his arms around his son and began to guide him toward the finish line. The father-and-son team crossed the finish line that day at the Barcelona Olympics to a standing ovation from the crowd. Jim's heroic act of helping his son finish the race resonated with fathers everywhere, and twenty years later, Jim Redmond was invited to carry the Olympic torch in the 2012 London Olympics.

So, let's dare to be great fathers like Jim Redmond! It is a challenge that requires tenacity, openness, clarity and courage. Let's attack being great fathers with even more ferocity than we attack our careers. Let's go after fathering with even more passion than we have for our local sports teams. Let's become aggressive and relentless learners about fatherhood—men who take themselves seriously and the calling of fatherhood seriously. In other words, let's be great fathers.

Enjoy the playbook!

Patrick E. Donohue

THE
PLAYBOOK

FATHERING TYPES

Every father is unique, but I would contend that there are six main fathering types: the *Wimp*, the *Volcano*, the *Talker*, the *Servant*, the *Pro* and the *Guru* (see the chart on the next page). All of us fathers have some of each category in us. Our own fathers can have dramatic influence on how we show up as fathers. For instance, if we were raised by a *Volcano* father, we can unconsciously bring those traits to our own fathering or we can go completely the other direction and become the *Wimp*. Our own self-awareness and positive action is what allows us to change styles. The key is to limit the first three categories (*Wimp, Volcano, Talker*) and increase the last three categories (*Servant, Pro, Guru*).

Read through these categories and reflect which of your children and/or situations bring out the different types in your fathering style. The second chart, Understanding the Plays, will serve as a guide as we look at the 48 plays. At the bottom of each play, there will be a football "wristband" that references two of the fathering styles.

Six Types of Fathers

The Type	Overheard	Shows Up as...	Effect on Children	Coaching Points
THE WIMP Apathetic, victim. Dad who just can't get stuff done, usually dislikes himself; has feelings of guilt, self-doubt, and fear, or feels like he has no power—often a nice guy who is not taken seriously by others.	"I feel so overwhelmed." "Nothing I do ever works." "These kids do not listen to me." "I am always so tired."	Low-energy father who is unengaged and cannot really be counted on. Spectator in his own life. Often seen as depressed or lethargic.	Children learn to work around dad because they cannot count on him, but secretly resent his lack of engagement. Dad's weakness can create an identity crisis in children who are waiting for him to lead.	Realize you have options, take responsibility for moving forward by taking consistent small steps forward.
THE VOLCANO Angry father, who is constantly stressed, frustrated and disappointed. Likes to compare his kids and sees life from a win-lose perspective; tends to blame others.	"Why can't anyone else do things right?" "That's not good enough." "Your brother would not do that." "There is never enough time."	Impatient father who is constantly preoccupied and stressed, likes to "teach lessons" by blaming and shaming the kids.	Children try to appease dad and make sure he does not get angry, or avoid him due to his erratic behavior.	Move past life as a win-lose paradigm, understand gray areas, manage outside stress and practice patience.

The Type	Overheard	Shows Up as...	Effect on Children	Coaching Points
THE TALKER The enthusiastic father who talks a big game, but does not always execute. Has good energy and is encouraging, but doesn't always have the plan to follow through and has many excuses.	"We tried, it just didn't work out." "I cannot wait until next season." "If I had not gotten sick, we would have done it."	Caring and encouraging father. Wants the best for his children. Big dreamer without a history of execution. Takes losses personally.	Younger children like being around the positive energy, older children can become disillusioned by the lack of follow through.	Need to stay enthusiastic and focus on executing on smaller things to build trust with children.
THE SERVANT Loving, caring father who wants the best for his kids. Empathetic and service-oriented to a fault; willing to do whatever it takes to help his kids. Can be manipulated by kids who take advantage of his kindness.	"I love helping my kids." "I will do anything for my kids." "I wonder if it will ever be my turn." "Being a dad is my most important job."	Compassionate father who consistently does things for his kids. Selfless and upbeat most of the time; problem solver; occasionally resents having to do all the dirty work.	Children feel important and secure around their father. They know he has their back at all times. Children can become demanding and entitled and treat father with a subtle lack of respect.	Great job making your children feel cared for, but it is also okay to challenge them and expect them to rise to the occasion. Also, important that the father keeps growing himself, not just becoming absorbed in kids activities.

The Type	Overheard	Shows Up as...	Effect on Children	Coaching Points
THE PRO Balanced father who coaches his kids with love and is unafraid to challenge them to greatness. Always thinking win-win for both the short- and long-term for his kids.	"We need to think this through for the long haul." "You are doing great and I know you have more in you."	Consistent father who is an anchor for his children. Listens empathetically, demands goal-setting and long-term thinking. Not afraid to have tough conversations.	Children know exactly what to expect from their father, so they grow exponentially in their security and sense of self. Children are willing to take risks because of the security of the father bond.	This is where we want to be as fathers. This father is totally engaged in his kids' lives, yet has interests of his own where he is growing and learning.
THE GURU The father who has moved completely beyond his own ego and dispenses wisdom as if he is Gandhi or Martin Luther King.	"What is the greater good in this situation?" "What will bring life to others?"	Father who is totally on another level. Comes across as a man of deep wisdom.	Children are mesmerized by this type of father, although they do not always understand him totally.	Guru level is a nice place to visit occasionally, but quite difficult to maintain. Appreciate the inspiration when it arrives.

Adapted from Bruce Schneider's type of leaders in *Energy Leadership*.

UNDERSTANDING THE PLAYS
Cheat Sheet

Term	What it Means
DEFINITION	Basic description of the football play that matches the diagram that is drawn.
OLD SCHOOL	An example of the play from college or pro football that goes back in time.
MODERN	An example of the play from college or pro football that is more recent.
THE SKINNY	The overall concept that ties the football play to a fathering challenge.
THE SITUATION	A scenario with a young child, preteen or teenager that requires action from a dad.
THE PLAY	The action a dad takes to effectively intervene in the situation.
COACH PAT'S PLAYBOOK	Thoughts, quotes and research findings from the author that are relevant to the play.
PENALTY FLAG	This is what not to do as a father. We don't want to be that guy.
WRISTBAND	References parts of the play back to the Six Types of Father chart.

FIRST QUARTER
The Basics

PLAY #1
Off Tackle Run

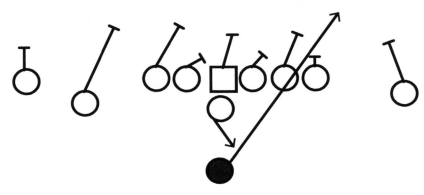

DEFINITION:
Basic play where the running back takes the ball and runs off the outside shoulder of the offensive tackle. Play is designed to pick up short, consistent yardage.

OLD SCHOOL: *Larry Cszonka,* Miami Dolphins
MODERN: *Adrian Peterson,* Minnesota Vikings

THE SKINNY:
The off tackle run is often used to keep the chains moving (picking up a first down). It is a basic, staple play that is run over and over to produce a predictable result.

THE SITUATION:
Your 13-year-old daughter seems to be a little off her game. Nothing terrible, but she just does not seem to be herself. She is a little quieter than normal and a little less into joking around. She seems preoccupied, like something is bothering her and maybe she doesn't even know why.

THE PLAY (GURU)

Every night you tuck your daughter into bed, even though she is not a little girl anymore. The routine usually lasts two or three minutes, but occasionally, when there is something bothering her, it lasts much longer. Your daughter explains that two of the girls at school are not being particularly nice to her. They have avoided her and said a couple of mean things about her. You have a nice chat about "real friendship" and how the only person we can control is ourselves. You finish the routine by kissing your daughter on the forehead.

COACH PAT'S PLAYBOOK

Bullying, whether it's done in-person or in cyberspace, is a major cause of anxiety and depression for middle school students. Kids will often withdraw before they admit that they are being bullied.

PENALTY FLAG: DON'T BE THAT GUY (TALKER)...

The father who embarrasses his daughter in front of the whole family by pointing out her behavior. Well-meaning attempts at humor like, "What's the matter Sarah, you look like someone stole your puppy," or, "You're so quiet, I almost forgot you were here," are not helpful. These attempts will drive your daughter further away from you.

WRISTBAND

The Play = Guru, the wise father
Penalty = Talker, the embarrassing father

PLAY #2
Fullback Lead Play

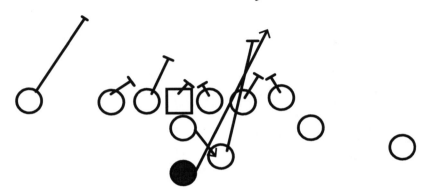

DEFINITION:
The fullback runs in front of the ball carrier and blocks anything in the way. His job is to create an opening for the ball carrier.

OLD SCHOOL: *Mike Alstott* blocking for *Warrick Dunn,* Tampa Bay Buccaneers
MODERN: *Vonta Leach* blocking for *Ray Rice,* Baltimore Ravens

THE SKINNY:
Sometimes with our kids, we have to show them the way by going in front of them and providing an example of how it is done.

THE SITUATION:
Your 11-year-old son is anxious to demonstrate his maturity by taking over the lawn-cutting duties from you. You have a large lawn that looks beautiful and you would like to keep it that way. He has watched you cut the lawn and has even mowed a few strips himself.

THE PLAY (PRO)

Start by explaining to your son what the finished product should look like. Cut the lawn yourself and have your child help, but mostly watch, you cut. Point out nuances, trouble spots and small tricks to him. Even have your son take notes to make sure he really understands what you are saying. The next week, help him get started by reviewing the notes and then turn him loose on the yard. When he is finished, walk around the yard with him and review the most important criteria. Remember to provide encouraging, constructive feedback on what he did well and matter-of-fact, nonjudgmental feedback on what could be better. Repeat the process one or two more times and your child will ace the lawn.

COACH PAT'S PLAYBOOK

Researcher Daniel Coyle says that the most powerful way to learn something new is to do it and the second most powerful way is to watch someone else do it. (Daniel Coyle, *The Talent Code*, p. 118).

PENALTY FLAG: DON'T BE THAT GUY (VOLCANO)...

The father who brings out the "white glove" and nothing will ever be good enough when he inspects the lawn. If you are turning over the lawn duty to your son, then realize he will not do it exactly the same way you would do it. If this is not okay, then do not turn over the duty. It is okay to have high standards, but perfectionism is not an acceptable target.

WRISTBAND

The Play = Pro, the teaching father
Penalty = Volcano, the perfectionist father

PLAY #3
Quick Opener

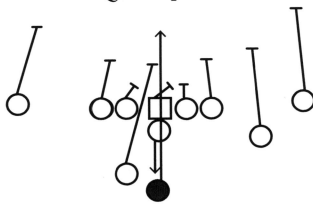

DEFINITION:
The running back takes an immediate hand off and smashes up the middle.

OLD SCHOOL: *Christian Okoye,* Kansas City Chiefs
MODERN: *Brandon Jacobs,* New York Giants

THE SKINNY:
Attacking a problem quickly and decisively can pay major dividends.

THE SITUATION:
Your 6-month-old daughter is still struggling to fall asleep and to sleep through the night. Everyone in the house is suffering from a lack of sleep and the tension is palpable. You are busy with tons of things to do, but you know that the current situation is not sustainable.

THE PLAY (SERVANT)

You fully tackle the sleeping issue. You get up with your daughter, but you also create "white noise" CDs and experiment with new sleeping positions and times. Your message to your wife is, "I got this one." Everyone wins.

COACH PAT'S PLAYBOOK

Being proactive rather than being reactive will score you major points as a father. Be aware of your environment and do things before you are asked to do them.

PENALTY FLAG: DON'T BE THAT GUY (WIMP)...

The father who becomes the martyr because he is losing a little sleep. Your strength or weakness as a father will impact the entire household.

WRISTBAND

The Play = Servant, the proactive father
Penalty = Wimp, the victim father

PLAY #4

Counter Play

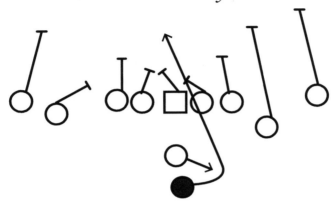

DEFINITION:
The running back jabs one direction and then takes the ball and runs the other direction.

OLD SCHOOL: *Barry Sanders,* Detroit Lions
MODERN: *Frank Gore,* San Francisco 49ers

THE SKINNY:
Going one direction and then quickly changing can be helpful. Fail fast and move on.

THE SITUATION:
Your 14-year-old son tries out for the baseball team and gets cut. He is heartbroken, because he has played baseball all his life. You come home and see him watching television in a daze.

THE PLAY (PRO)

Talk with your son and help him process the disappointment in as rational a manner as possible. Acknowledge his grief and disappointment, but also point out that when disappointment and turmoil come to our lives, it often creates opportunity. Remind him of all the great qualities and talents that he possesses. Start the process of brainstorming what your son might be able to do with the time he was going to commit to baseball. Perhaps he could get a job, volunteer, join a school club or even try out for another sport. Remind him that the most successful people in life are the ones who fail, learn from it and keep going.

COACH PAT'S PLAYBOOK

Failing at something is an event. Being a "failure" is an identity. It is important to keep these two concepts completely separate.

PENALTY FLAG: DON'T BE THAT GUY (VOLCANO)...

The father who shames his son by talking about how he should have been more prepared for the tryout in the middle of the son's grief. This father will often refuse to acknowledge his son's disappointment and basically tells him to "man up" and get over it.

WRISTBAND

The Play = Pro, the reflective father
Penalty = Volcano, the shaming father

PLAY #5

Bootleg

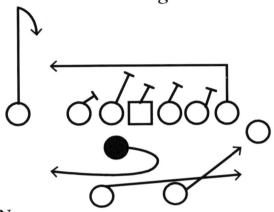

DEFINITION:
The entire action of a play goes one way and the QB fakes that way and reverses out the other direction in order to create more space and opportunity.

OLD SCHOOL: *Randall Cunningham,* Philadelphia Eagles/
Minnesota Vikings
MODERN: *Robert Griffin III,* Washington Redskins

THE SKINNY:
Reversing course on a decision is sometimes the best move you can make.

THE SITUATION:
Your third child is 11 and begging you for a cell phone. She points out how it could be a safety and communication tool for her. Your previous two children did not get cell phones until they were 12 and that has been the family rule.

THE PLAY (PRO)

You and your spouse talk it over and realize that the world has changed a little bit in the last five years since your older kids first got cell phones. It is now common for eight-year-olds to have cell phones. Does your daughter absolutely "need" a cell phone at age eleven? Probably not, but the downside of having her feel isolated from her peers and angry at you is not worth it. Get her the cell phone, set responsible parameters that she has to follow and explain to your older children that making adjustments are part of life.

COACH PAT'S PLAYBOOK

Stubbornly sticking to principles even when they have become outdated or nonsensical is a formula to alienate your children.

PENALTY FLAG: DON'T BE THAT GUY (VOLCANO)...

The father who is unwilling to reconsider any decision and sees any discussion as a threat to his authority. This type of father will occasionally change his mind, but he secretly resents it and tries to make his children forever feel guilty.

WRISTBAND

The Play = Pro, the flexible father
Penalty = Volcano, the dictatorial father

PLAY #6

Quick Pitch

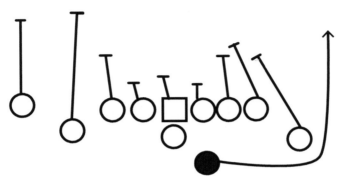

DEFINITION:
The quarterback pitches the ball to the tailback who runs around the end.

OLD SCHOOL: *Billy Sims,* Detroit Lions
MODERN: *Terrell Davis,* Denver Broncos

THE SKINNY:
Sometimes just getting outside is what needs to happen.

THE SITUATION:
Your first-grade son is bouncing off the walls and driving his mother crazy. You receive a call on your way home from work that things are not going well. You arrive home from work and can sense the tension in the house and see the mess that has been created.

THE PLAY (SERVANT)

Greet your wife and immediately grab your son and take him outside for 30 to 45 minutes. Let him burn off some energy, but also ask him about how things were going in the home. Help him to self-reflect and see that his behavior was frustrating to his mother. Come back in the house and supervise or help him clean up the mess he has created.

COACH PAT'S PLAYBOOK

Talking to boys while they are active is an excellent strategy. You will have a much deeper conversation with the average boy on a walk rather than at the kitchen table.

PENALTY FLAG: DON'T BE THAT GUY (TALKER)...

The father who talks with his son and then forces a disingenuous apology to his mother. Insincere apologies are a waste of time.

WRISTBAND

The Play = Servant, the active father
Penalty = Talker, the self-righteous father

PLAY #7

Power Sweep

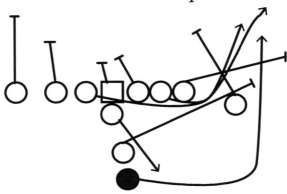

DEFINITION:
The quarterback pitches/hands off to the tailback who runs wide behind a wall of blockers including the fullback and pulling linemen.

OLD SCHOOL: Green Bay Packers 1960s
MODERN: USC Trojans Power Sweep (Student Body Right)

THE SKINNY:
Sometimes we need to get out in front of our kids and support them with a lot of resources.

THE SITUATION:
You have three children and your youngest daughter, a 7th grader, is having a difficult time with the team of teachers she has this year. The teachers are demanding and not particularly nurturing. You daughter is performing poorly, and her confidence level has taken a big hit.

THE PLAY (PRO)

It's time to have the entire family get involved to help your daughter. You enlist your older daughter, an 11th grader, to talk with her younger sister about the ups and downs of middle school. You talk to your 8th grade son to check in with his sister once a day at school. You talk with your daughter and see if the services of a tutor or coach might be helpful. You and your wife build her confidence by reminding her of all her great qualities and give her opportunities to serve others.

COACH PAT'S PLAYBOOK

The most important thing we can do during a difficult periods for our kids is to reassure them that the difficulty is temporary, not permanent.

PENALTY FLAG: DON'T BE THAT GUY (VOLCANO)...

The father who sends high-handed and threatening emails to the school about the situation with his daughter. Nobody likes to be blindsided, including teachers. If you think a meeting with the teachers is warranted, then set it up and proceed in a calm manner.

WRISTBAND

The Play = Pro, the leader father
Penalty = Volcano, the threatening father

PLAY #8

Scissors Counter Trap

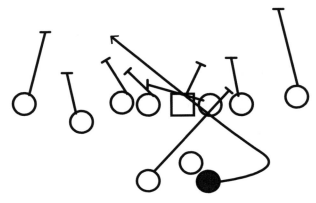

DEFINITION:
Split backfield and the two running backs cross with the ball being faked to the first back and the second back getting the ball.

OLD SCHOOL: *Greg Pruitt*, Cleveland Browns
MODERN: Nebraska Cornhuskers

THE SKINNY:
Appearing to go one direction, but actually planning on going the other direction can be a great strategy.

THE SITUATION:
You and your wife have planned a family outing with your seven- and five-year-old sons to go to a local park and take a hike. The boys are moderately excited, but not thrilled about the outing. They are boys who appreciate adventure.

THE PLAY (PRO)

Talk to your wife about one last trip to the local amusement park for the year. Buy the tickets and do not say anything to your sons. Get in the car and start driving towards the amusement park and have your wife ask, "Where are we going?" Pull out the tickets to the amusement park and get ready to hear the cheers.

COACH PAT'S PLAYBOOK

It is called a surprise for a reason. This is a play that can only be run once in awhile to have maximum impact.

PENALTY FLAG: DON'T BE THAT GUY (TALKER)...

The father who pulls out surprises every week, so that the surprises are not fun, they are disruptive. Too many surprises is code for chaos.

WRISTBAND

The Play = Pro, the clever father
Penalty = Talker, the overkill father

PLAY #9

QB Waggle

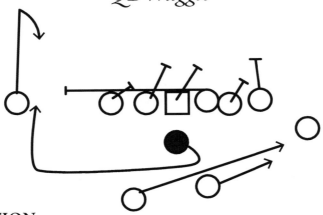

DEFINITION:
The quarterback fakes to the running back and then sprints to the end with a run/pass option.

OLD SCHOOL: *Steve Young,* San Francisco 49ers
MODERN: *Michael Vick,* Philadelphia Eagles

THE SKINNY:
Being flexible and having more than one way to attack is always helpful.

THE SITUATION:
Your fourth-grade daughter is anxious about a huge project that is due for class. This project requires some combination of writing, art and use of technology. She is frozen with fear of making a mistake and not getting a good grade. She talks about not being "smart enough" to do a good job on the project.

THE PLAY (PRO)

Start by reassuring her that you will help her get through the project. Break the project down with her and lay out the different options. Tell her that there is no one singular way to do the project successfully. Become a team with her and coach her through the project. Set up a schedule to complete the project, but be flexible to make adjustments.

COACH PAT'S PLAYBOOK

Helping our children chunk large projects into smaller parts is a formula for success and for overcoming procrastination.

PENALTY FLAG: DON'T BE THAT GUY (VOLCANO)...

The father becomes impatient with his daughter's hesitation and fear. When we are impatient, we reinforce the notion that our child is not good enough.

WRISTBAND

The Play = Pro, the collaborative father
Penalty = Volcano, the impatient father

PLAY #10

Stretch Run

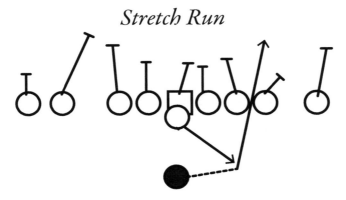

DEFINITION:
Basic handoff to the tailback who waits, waits, waits for the hole to open up, reads the situation and then hits the hole squarely.

OLD SCHOOL: *Marcus Allen,* Oakland Raiders
MODERN: *Arian Foster,* Houston Texans

THE SKINNY:
This is "the talk" with dad that everyone knows is coming after an incident has happened. This talk can either move your relationship forward or stall it.

THE SITUATION:
Your 13-year-old son gets caught cheating on a test at school and is given no credit from the teacher. The teacher leaves you a voice message indicating that she caught him trying to cheat. You are not able to reach the teacher before you arrive home. Your wife has indicated that your son is nervously pacing around the house, waiting for your return.

THE PLAY (GURU)

Take a deep breath on the commute home and compose yourself with some positive thoughts about your son. As you enter the house, your mantra is "let the play come to me." Greet your son and give him an opening by asking, "How was your day at school?" He might actually tell you about the incident at that point. If he doesn't talk about the cheating, mention that you received a voice message from his teacher. Again, like a good tailback on the stretch play, let the play develop in front of you. Let him tell you about the incident in his own words. Your job is to wait and ask open-ended questions about what happened—and more importantly, why it happened.

The real value of this conversation is to figure out why your son felt compelled to cheat. What underlying pressure is he feeling and how can you help alleviate that pressure? You want to communicate that you love your son no matter what and there is no need to cheat. Help him deal with underlying identity issue as well as attack the challenges around organization, priorities and how to study.

COACH PAT'S PLAYBOOK

The energy level a conversation starts with is typically how it will end. If you want to end on a positive note, then start on a positive note.

PENALTY FLAG: DON'T BE THAT GUY (VOLCANO)...

The father enters the house and immediately makes a sarcastic, shaming remark about the cheating incident. Comments like, "I never had to cheat" or "I don't know how you could be so stupid" or "What is going on in your brain?" are not helpful. They will set a negative tone and most likely spur an unproductive conversation. These fathers tend to overreact and then wonder why their kids will not open up to them later.

WRISTBAND

The Play = Guru, the patient father
Penalty = Volcano, the condescending father

PLAY #11

Dive

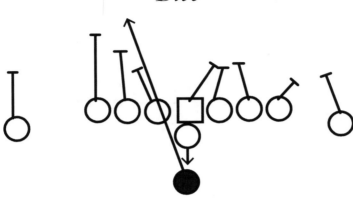

DEFINITION:
Halfback or fullback takes the handoff and goes straight up the middle.

OLD SCHOOL: *John Riggins,* Redskins
MODERN: *Lorenzo Neal, Bucaneers,* Broncos, Chargers

THE SKINNY:
The most basic play that every offense must have and must know how to execute.

THE SITUATION:
Your six-year-old, athletic daughter comes home from kindergarten crying and says she never wants to go to gym class again.

THE PLAY (PRO)

Start by giving your daughter a hug and hold her until she settles down. Let her vent her concerns and then slowly start to ask her for details. You will most likely find out that she got physically hurt, embarrassed or somehow isolated in the class. Talk to her about how to handle those situations. Remind her of all the great times she has had in gym class previously. Close by telling her you think she is awesome and give her another hug.

COACH PAT'S PLAYBOOK

One of our main jobs as fathers is to provide safety and reassurance for our children. This means physically (hugs) and emotionally (listening intently).

PENALTY FLAG: DON'T BE THAT GUY (WIMP)...

The father who tells his daughter not to cry and not to be upset. Feelings do not get processed by invalidating them on the front end.

WRISTBAND

The Play = Pro, the empathetic father
Penalty = Wimp, the avoiding father

PLAY #12

Man in Motion

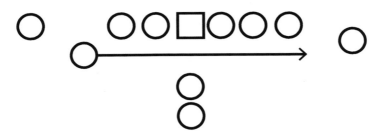

DEFINITION:
Typically a receiver or running back will run parallel to the line of scrimmage before the ball is snapped in order to gain a positional advantage.

OLD SCHOOL: San Diego Chargers "Air Coryell"
MODERN: *Peyton Manning,* Indianapolis Colts

THE SKINNY:
New positioning can create new opportunities.

THE SITUATION:
Your 15-year-old son is struggling in school. Each night you typically poke your head into his room and check on his homework. Inevitably, those conversations turn negative and take on the form of an interrogation. Your son becomes defensive and you feel like a police officer. Nobody feels good after these discussions.

THE PLAY (GURU)

Time to go in motion, literally. Stop talking to your son about school in his room. Change the vibe and the messaging. Casually ask him about school when you pick him up or when you are just watching TV together. Look for smaller opportunities to discuss his school work in a less head-on, onerous setting. Walk to the store or pharmacy together and just have school come up as one of several discussion points.

COACH PAT'S PLAYBOOK

Most teenagers respond best to their parents when the discussion is focused, but not totally direct. A distraction, like being in the car, watching TV or being at a ballgame can provide the room for a teen to feel emotionally safe.

PENALTY FLAG: DON'T BE THAT GUY (TALKER)...

The father who talks about how much homework he did as a kid and doesn't understand why this is so hard. Referencing the good old days as a way to make a negative comparison is never a good idea.

WRISTBAND

The Play = Guru, the sensitive father
Penalty = Talker, the comparing father

END OF FIRST QUARTER

Sideline Reporter

HAVE YOU EVER MET A DISAPPOINTED FATHER? I am not talking about the father who is down once in awhile about his children. I am talking about the father who is perpetually criticizing or nitpicking his children. This is the father whose kid gets six "A"s and one "B+" and the father does not acknowledge the hard work for the six "A"s, he only wants to harp about the "B+". This is the father whose kid makes 15 tackles in a football game, but misses a couple of tackles, and the dad chooses to focus on the misses.

Some of us were raised in this type of environment. So, what is the long-term consequence of this type of fathering? Well, the good news is your children will probably achieve well, because they feel overwhelming pressure to do so. The bad news is they will most likely feel inadequate and spend their life trying to prove themselves to you and others.

Great fathers acknowledge the accomplishments of their children and validate their feelings. We need to move away from the nonsense of "don't compliment them or they will get a big head" and move toward the mantra of "celebration, challenge and growth." Great fathers understand that kids need a combination of encouragement and nudging to reach their full potential.

The disappointed father reveals more about his own personal outlook than feelings about his children, while the great father is totally engaged and in-tune with the emotional needs of his children.

SECOND QUARTER

To the Air

PLAY #13

Comeback Route

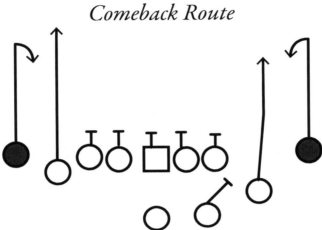

DEFINITION:
Wide receiver goes 10-15 yards down the field, turns, plants and comes back towards the quarterback in order to catch the ball.

OLD SCHOOL: *Fred Bilitnekoff,* Oakland Raiders
MODERN: *Chris Carter,* Minnesota Vikings

THE SKINNY:
The idea is to meet your son where he is, rather than where you want him to be. This means moving towards his interests rather than forcing your interests on him.

THE SITUATION:
Your 13-year-old son is a compliant kid who has played athletics his whole life with middling success. You have coached him, paid for private lessons and cheered him on for years. Now, as he enters high school, he is talking about how he would love to pursue art and music and he is not so sure about athletics. He has talked about not trying out for athletic teams and pursuing other club activities.

THE PLAY (PRO)

This can be tough, especially for the dad who has a strong athletic identity himself. But this is not about you, Dad, or the money spent on lessons, travel teams or equipment. This is about your son pursuing his passion. Start by sitting down with your son and discussing not only his interest in art and music, but also his hesitancy on continuing with sports. Communicate that you want him to pursue his passions, but also challenge him to think his decision all the way through. Ultimately, the message you want to communicate is "I want you going full speed and full commitment at things you are interested in." On quitting sports, make sure your son is running towards something (art, music), rather than running away from something (failure in sports).

COACH PAT'S PLAYBOOK

As Sir Kenneth Robinson, British educational philosopher said: "We are in our element at the intersection of what we are good at and what we like to do."

PENALTY FLAG: DON'T BE THAT GUY (VOLCANO)...

The father who cannot give up his dream for his son to be a star high school athlete and forces the young man to keep playing sports even when his ability and passion have both clearly waned. The son is likely to feign injuries or sickness in order to avoid the pain of disappointing his father. This is the father who finds out years later that his son secretly resented him.

WRISTBAND

The Play = Pro, the balanced father
Penalty = Volcano, the tone-deaf father

PLAY #14

Max Protection

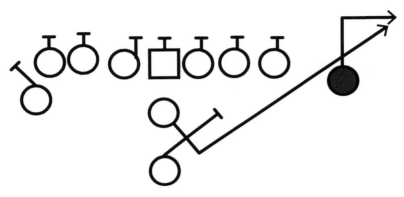

DEFINITION:

The offense keeps a tight end and a running back in to protect the quarterback and sends only one or two guys into the pass pattern.

OLD SCHOOL: *Bill Parcells,* New York Giants
MODERN: *Jim Harbaugh,* San Francisco 49ers

THE SKINNY:

When safety is the issue, it is time to go into max protection mode.

THE SITUATION:

Your 17-year-old daughter has asked to go to a party at someone's house who lives in another town. You agree to this, but tell her that if she is at all uncomfortable to text you immediately. At 9:30 pm, you receive a text saying, "Party is pretty loud." You write back, "Are you OK?" She writes back, "I guess."

THE PLAY (SERVANT)

Call your daughter immediately and see what is going on. If you sense at all that she is uncomfortable or scared, go and pick her up right away. You can even pick her up a couple of houses down from the party to avoid the "Dad just picked me up" stigma. Use the car ride as a time to debrief the party. Ask her why she seemed uncomfortable. Tell her you appreciate her being responsible and that you love her.

COACH PAT'S PLAYBOOK

Read between the lines on communication and do not focus on the exact words. Your daughter is not texting you that the party is "pretty loud" just to give you a status update —she is concerned.

PENALTY FLAG: DON'T BE THAT GUY (WIMP)...

The father ignores all emotional cues and focuses only on the exact words being communicated. Later, this father will say, "I didn't know she was worried, she just said the party was loud."

WRISTBAND

The Play = Servant, the concerned father
Penalty = Wimp, the excuse-making father

PLAY #15

Hook Pattern

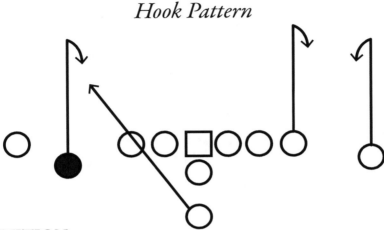

DEFINITION:
Receiver runs an 8-10 yard pattern and then turns back towards the quarterback in order to catch the ball.

OLD SCHOOL: *Steve Largent,* Seattle Seahawks
MODERN: *Wes Welker,* New England Patriots/Denver Broncos

THE SKINNY:
The hook is a safe play, but it is called "hook" for a reason. The receiver "hooks" the quarterback's interest by coming back to the ball.

THE SITUATION:
You and your wife will be out of town at the same time, so your 14-year-old son is going to have to come on a three-day business trip with you. He is reluctant to come because he will be missing the annual festival in your town. He has asked why he can't just stay at a friends house, rather than go on a "dumb old business trip."

THE PLAY (PRO)

Time to find a hook for your son. Sit down with him and excitedly research the area you are going to together. Start planning every meal, every excursion and even what you want to have for snacks. Take a virtual tour of the hotel and see what amenities are available. Send him text messages with new ideas as the trip approaches and plan one large outing like a ballgame, amusement park or go-cart race that he will enjoy.

COACH PAT'S PLAYBOOK

When a father is enthusiastic about an idea, event or trip, it affects the mood of the entire family.

PENALTY FLAG: DON'T BE THAT GUY (VOLCANO)...

The father who starts arguing with his son and telling him why he is not staying at his friend's house. This father insinuates that the son is not trustworthy.

WRISTBAND

The Play = Pro, the planning father
Penalty = Volcano, the passive-aggressive father

PLAY #16

Quick Slant

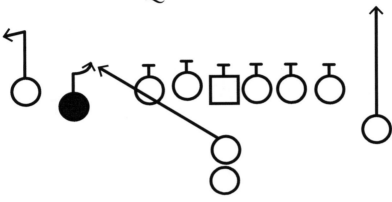

DEFINITION:
The receiver runs about 5 yards and turns in and looks to catch the ball in rhythm, so he can get a larger gain.

OLD SCHOOL: *Jerry Rice,* San Francisco 49ers
MODERN: *Calvin Johnson,* Detroit Lions

THE SKINNY:
A well-placed, small gesture can lead to much bigger gains.

THE SITUATION:
Your 13-year-old daughter is struggling with the start of her 8th grade year. She is complaining that she has no friends and that she hates school. You know that the acne on her face is really a discouraging development for her. It's mid-September, so it is looking like it could be a long year.

THE PLAY (GURU)

Grab your daughter's lunch box or backpack and put a short hand-written note in it that describes one awesome characteristic that she possesses. A couple of days later do the same thing with an inspiring quote. Randomly continue this pattern for a month.

COACH PAT'S PLAYBOOK

The subconscious mind is like a scale. The things we hear the most, weigh the most and thus have the most impact. Reinforcing the positive on a daily basis is key to changing our mindset.

PENALTY FLAG: DON'T BE THAT GUY (VOLCANO)...

The father who writes one note and then is upset when there is not an immediate change. To change a mindset takes patience and persistence.

WRISTBAND

The Play = Guru, the encouraging father
Penalty = Volcano, the unrealistic father

PLAY #17
Check Down Pass

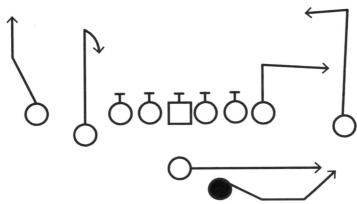

DEFINITION:
The quarterback is looking for his star receiver down the field, but he is double covered, so he "checks down" and passes to his running back coming out of the backfield.

OLD SCHOOL: *Joe Montana,* San Francisco 49ers
MODERN: *Tom Brady,* New England Patriots

THE SKINNY:
A willingness to go to Plan B when the first option is not working is a sign of wisdom.

THE SITUATION:
Every year your entire family goes to the local amusement park and has a great time. You typically arrive when the park opens and stay all the way until the park closes. This year the date has been changed because of another conflict and your elementary school-aged kids are just coming back from a week at camp. The night before you go, there is arguing and bickering that you know can be mainly attributed to everyone being exhausted.

THE PLAY (PRO)

You have a bad feeling that the normal great day at the amusement park might turn into a nightmare. The night before you propose three other possible options: 1) Sleeping in and going to the park in the afternoon. 2) Going to the beach in the afternoon and eating at a local burger joint. 3) Chilling at home all day and going out for a nice family meal. Be open to variations of these three options or even something totally different.

COACH PAT'S PLAYBOOK

Lack of sleep is a major concern for most American teenagers. The average American teenager would benefit from 8-10 hours of sleep, but most only get 6-8 hours of sleep. (Mayo Clinic Tween and Teen Health blog: *Why is Your Teen so Tired?*).

PENALTY FLAG: DON'T BE THAT GUY (VOLCANO)...

The father who will not change plans, because we are going to "have fun" no matter what happens. This father becomes angry at his children for being tired and ruining their big family day.

WRISTBAND

The Play = Pro, the creative father
Penalty = Volcano, the stubborn father

PLAY #18

Bubble Screen

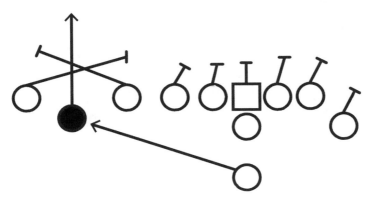

DEFINITION:
A quick pass at the line of scrimmage to give the receiver some space to make a big play.

OLD SCHOOL: *Raghib "Rocket" Ismail,* Notre Dame
MODERN: *Percy Harvin,* Minnesota Vikings/Seattle Seahawks

THE SKINNY:
Giving our kids space to operate is key to their success.

THE SITUATION:
Your 15-year-old daughter has taken to coloring her hair a different color each week and wearing outfits that you find hideous. The outfits are not inappropriate or overly revealing, just mismatched and not stylish from your point of view.

THE PLAY (PRO)

Time to give your daughter some space to grow. As long as her outfits are not sexually inappropriate or unsafe, and her hair color can be washed out, let her experiment. Teenagers need to discover their own style and identity. When we become too restrictive, we send the message that we do not trust our kids and they will most likely go underground to quietly rebel against us. Remember, many of us had some bad feathered hair in the 80s and ugly mullets in the 90s.

COACH PAT'S PLAYBOOK

Being in total control of our child's fashion and hairstyle is like trying to hold a ball underwater. Eventually the ball will rise to the surface and pop out. Every battle is not worth fighting.

PENALTY FLAG: DON'T BE THAT GUY (TALKER)...

The father who has a daily critique of his daughter's hairstyle and dress. This is a no-win situation where alienation and tension are the most likely outcomes. On the other hand, do not be the clueless father who never acknowledges when his daughter changes her hairstyle or dress.

WRISTBAND

The Play = Pro, the open father
Penalty = Talker, the critical father

PLAY #19

Shallow Cross

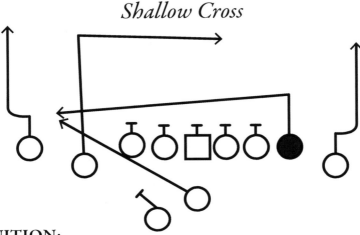

DEFINITION:

The quarterback drops back to pass and hits either the tight end or receiver who crosses the field and "sits down" in an area that is open.

OLD SCHOOL: *Tom Waddle,* Chicago Bears
MODERN: *Wes Welker,* New England Patriots/Denver Broncos

THE SKINNY:

Where we physically locate ourselves or "sit down" in the house makes a difference for our children.

THE SITUATION:

Your two-year-old son loves to touch everything, bang on tables and stand on the couch. He needs consistent supervision and loves to take things out. In other words, he is just being a normal active two-year old.

THE PLAY (SERVANT)

Time for you as a dad to physically sit down in the living room or wherever your son is hanging out. You might be watching the ballgame or answering emails, but now is the time to make a difference just with your presence.

COACH PAT'S PLAYBOOK

The best discipline method whether at home or in a school is proximity. When we are physically close to our children, they are much less likely to misbehave.

PENALTY FLAG: DON'T BE THAT GUY (WIMP)...

The father who is in the room with his toddler, but pays no attention and the kid is running wild. Supervision means we are actually paying attention to our child.

WRISTBAND

The Play = Servant, the present father
Penalty = Wimp, the unaware father

PLAY #20

Hot Receiver

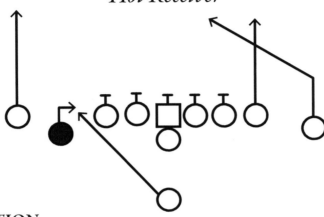

DEFINITION:

The defense sends a blitz and the quarterback throws to a receiver who is immediately open, often where the blitzer has vacated.

OLD SCHOOL: *John Taylor,* San Francisco 49ers
MODERN: *Oz Hakeem,* St. Louis Rams

THE SKINNY:

It is critical to know where the pressure points are in our homes and take action accordingly.

THE SITUATION:

You have your monthly dinner date set up with your 15-year-old son. Both of you are looking forward to going to the local diner. Meanwhile, your 13-year-old daughter is distraught because she did not receive a part in the school play and has been asked to be on the stage crew.

THE PLAY (GURU)

Ask your son if you can bump his time back and go for dessert or switch to a new day. Immediately sit down with your daughter and help her process her feelings about the play rejection. Listen quietly as she vents. Point out that the damage is not permanent and that working on the stage crew could be a lot of fun and a great learning experience.

COACH PAT'S PLAYBOOK

Teenagers can be quite emotional, yet most are not great at understanding their emotions. A few well-placed, open-ended questions can help your teen unlock his or her emotions and release the gas bubble in their tummies!

PENALTY FLAG: DON'T BE THAT GUY (WIMP)...

The father who tells his daughter she should not be upset and thereby invalidates her feelings. This strategy is often used by fathers who avoid conflict, but it tends to worsen situations.

WRISTBAND

The Play = Guru, the understanding father
Penalty = Wimp, the avoiding father

PLAY #21

Spiking the Ball

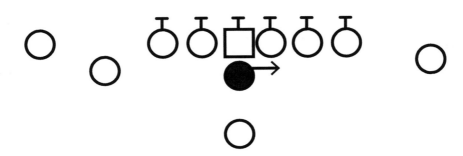

DEFINITION:
Quarterback rushes up to the line of scrimmage, takes the snap and spikes the ball into the ground in order to quickly and efficiently stop the clock.

OLD SCHOOL: *Dan Marino,* Miami Dolphins
MODERN: *Peyton Manning,* Indianapolis Colts/Denver Broncos

THE SKINNY:
Sometimes stepping in quickly to help your child is the best, most efficient play for everyone involved.

THE SITUATION:
Your 16-year-old son is struggling to get a job application filled out that is due tomorrow. It is the first time he has filled out a job application and he does not really understand the intent of the questions. He is struggling to complete the application and does not fully appreciate the urgency of turning in the application.

THE PLAY (SERVANT)

Now is the time to step in and help your son complete the application. Let him stay at the computer, but it is your job to go through the application question by question with him and work through the answers. Do not give him the answers, but ask the right leading questions that will help him understand the intent of the questions. Stress to your son that the application is the first impression you will make on a potential employer, so it is important.

COACH PAT'S PLAYBOOK

Most people procrastinate on things where they are afraid of rejection or failure. Facing the fear is the first step in ending through the cycle of procrastination. Once the fear has been identified, then breaking the task down into elemental parts can provide momentum to get it done.

PENALTY FLAG: DON'T BE THAT GUY (TALKER)...

The father who spends 30 minutes lecturing his son about the evils of procrastination as the clock continues to tick on the application being due. This father is likely to sit down and take over the computer and do the entire application for his son. The son gets the message that he is not capable and the father is resentful, thinking that he always has to do everything.

WRISTBAND

The Play = Servant, the prioritizing father
Penalty = Talker, the self-righteous father

PLAY #22

Wheel Route

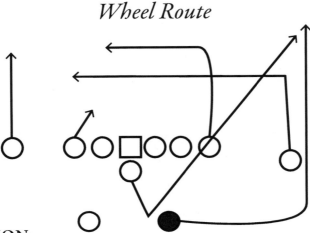

DEFINITION:
The quarterback drops back to pass and the tailback runs a flat route that he turns upfield and catches a deep pass.

OLD SCHOOL: *Chuck Foreman,* Minnesota Viking
MODERN: *Reggie Bush,* New Orleans Saints/Maimi Dolphins/Detroit Lions

THE SKINNY:
Starting out with a short conversation and then going deep is a great way to connect with our kids.

THE SITUATION:
Your 4th grade daughter is an excellent soccer player. She is the leading scorer on her team, but she sometimes feels like some of the other girls are jealous of her. Your daughter just wants to be friends with her teammates. She is tempted to not try as hard so she will fit in more with the girls.

THE PLAY (PRO)

Sit down with your daughter at a comfortable place and time and ask her about soccer. Start by talking about her performance and how proud you are of the skill and effort she is developing. As the conversation gets going, take it deeper by asking about the reaction of the other girls to her play. Remind your daughter that jealousy is not her problem, it is the issue of the other girls. Your daughter is not responsible for their feelings.

COACH PAT'S PLAYBOOK

Co-dependency, or feeling responsible for other people's feelings, can be crippling. On our best day, the only person we can control is ourselves. We are not responsible for other people's feelings, no matter what the circumstances.

PENALTY FLAG: DON'T BE THAT GUY (WIMP)...

The father who only talks with his daughter about what a great player she is avoids any emotional issues. This father might also badmouth other players in order to support his daughter.

WRISTBAND

The Play = Pro, the connecting father
Penalty = Wimp, the cowardly father

PLAY #23

The Fade Pattern

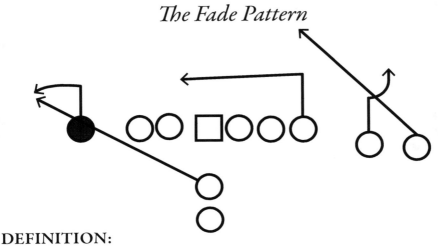

DEFINITION:

The quarterbacks lofts a pass high to the receiver where only he can catch the ball, usually to score a touchdown or get a first down.

OLD SCHOOL: *Randy Moss,* Minnesota Viking
MODERN: *Calvin Johnson,* Detroit Lions

THE SKINNY:

The fade pattern takes a deft touch from the quarterback and trust that his receiver will go and get the ball. The QB needs to put the ball in a place for the receiver to succeed.

THE SITUATION:

Your 18-year-old son wants to take your family car on a spring break road trip with several buddies. The friends are boys you know well and trust for the most part, but their ultimate destination is ten hours away.

THE PLAY (PRO)

You sit down with your son and have him explain the plan for the trip. You do not need to micromanage every detail, but you need to ask pointed questions about safety, money, communication, lodging and drug/alcohol issues. Like a good fade pattern, you need to put things in a position where your son can succeed. Once you are comfortable with the plan, you need to step back and trust your son to execute it, while providing a level of backup support. If you are not comfortable with the plan, time for an audible.

COACH PAT'S PLAYBOOK

"Letting go doesn't mean that you don't care about someone anymore. It's just realizing that the only person you really have control over is yourself."

– Deborah Reber, *Chicken Soup for the Teenage Soul*

PENALTY FLAG: DON'T BE THAT GUY (TALKER)...

The father who needs to micromanage every rest stop and decide which fast food restaurants are best. This father squeezes the joy and independence out of the trip by completely taking over the planning process.

WRISTBAND

The Play = Pro, the respectful father
Penalty = Talker, the micromanaging father

PLAY #24

Fly Pattern

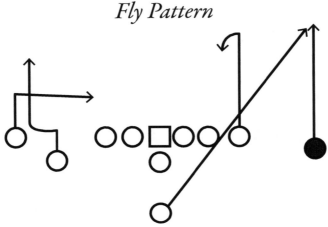

DEFINITION:
Receiver runs straight down the field looking to catch a deep pass from the quarterback who is looking to go for it.

OLD SCHOOL: *Bob Hayes,* Dallas Cowboys
MODERN: *Cliff Branch,* Oakland Raiders

THE SKINNY:
Being totally committed and going for it can pay off big.

THE SITUATION:
Your 18-year-old has a chance to get an internship at a prestigious engineering firm. He is a bright kid, but he has never really interviewed for anything. He is a low-key kid who tends to downplay his ability and minimize his accomplishments. His interview is in two days.

THE PLAY (SERVANT)

Talk to your son about "coaching" him through the interview process. Point out basics like posture, eye contact and keeping his answers brief, then start the mock interview process. Pepper him with questions you think he might get during the interview. In a gentle and constructive way, help him make improvements. Do the mock interviews for about 40 minutes for two nights in a row.

COACH PAT'S PLAYBOOK

Practice that simulates game like conditions is the best way to prepare for an athletic contest, job interview or even a difficult conversation. Rehearsal is definitely not overrated.

PENALTY FLAG: DON'T BE THAT GUY (VOLCANO)...

The father who never points out what is going well in the interview process, only mistakes. All human beings thrive on making a sense of forward progress.

WRISTBAND

The Play = Servant, the rehearsing father
Penalty = Volcano, the critical father

MY DAUGHTER WAS 13-YEARS-OLD WHEN SHE SQUARELY PUT ME IN MY PLACE. We were having a conversation and I was being a little silly and not taking her seriously. She announced, "Dad you still treat me like I am a little girl! I am not 9-years-old anymore!"

Ouch!

After I recovered from the sting of her statement, I realized she was right. I liked her when she was nine and had locked her into that age, moving forward. The teenage years felt a little too complex and edgy for me. I liked the simplicity of the compliant 9-year-old daughter, but that was not helping my daughter.

She was actually a quite mature 13-year-old, so I was really treating her below her age. After that fateful rebuke, I made a decision to intentionally develop a more mature and deep relationship with my daughter. It started simply with daddy-daughter dates to the local Boston Market. This became our go-to place, where only she and I went together. We had free-flowing conversations about school, spirituality, boys, drugs, sex and friends. I even discovered that some of our best conversations happened in the car, even before we got to Boston Market. We added other activities and traditions and now we have a relationship that both of us feel good about.

My lesson? Let your kids grow up. It is not as scary as you think and it is actually more fun than I could have imagined.

THIRD QUARTER

Defense, Special Teams
& Pressure Situations

PLAY #25
Bump & Run Coverage

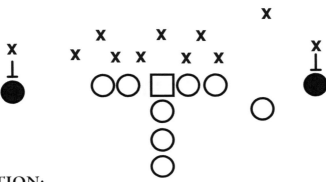

DEFINITION:
Aggressive man-to-man coverage strategy that is used to disrupt a threatening wide receiver.

OLD SCHOOL: *Lester Hayes,* Oakland Raiders
MODERN: *Richard Sherman,* Seattle Seahawks

THE SKINNY:
Sometimes fathering calls for an up-close-and-personal approach. No time to sit back: time to get right into the fray and dictate the action.

THE SITUATION:
Your 14-year-old daughter has a new group of friends in high school. These girls appear to be a little more "worldly" and boy-crazy than the friends you are used to. You are concerned as you watch your daughter become more and more obsessed with her appearance. She has also become more secretive around the house with her texting and Facebook usage. She seems to be focused on boys in an unhealthy way.

THE PLAY (PRO)

Time to get right on the line of scrimmage of your daughter's life and find out what is going on. This takes a combination of subtlety, tenacity and wisdom. Meet her new friends and get to know them by offering to be the parent that gives rides. It is amazing what you can learn just listening in the car. Go out of your way to connect one-on-one with your daughter and find out what is important to her. If she likes chocolate, have a brief talk over a bag of M&Ms. If she loves art, then find an art store, art museum, arty pictures — anything arty to connect about. Most young girls seek male attention when they feel like they have not received enough male attention at home. Time to change the attention deficit into an attention surplus. Your whole strategy needs to be deliberate, yet not strangely obvious.

COACH PAT'S PLAYBOOK

When a daughter is not sure of her father's affection, she will often find other males to affirm her personality, intelligence or beauty.

PENALTY FLAG: DON'T BE THAT GUY (VOLCANO)...

The father who swoops in and attempts to control his daughter's every behavior. This dad goes nuts and shuts down the cell phone, Facebook and contact with friends or a boyfriend. This strategy might gain short-term compliance, but it will backfire in the end. You have moved from bump and run coverage to pass interference.

WRISTBAND

The Play = Pro, the proactive father
Penalty = Volcano, the controlling father

PLAY #26
Onside Kick

DEFINITION:
A short squib kick-off done with the intent of the kicking team recovering the ball. This is usually done as a surprise tactic or a desperation tactic at the end of a game.

OLD SCHOOL: Pittsburgh Steelers, Super Bowl XXX
MODERN: New Orleans Saints, Super Bowl XLIV

THE SKINNY:
The surprise onside kick is a high risk, high-reward tactic that can be really powerful in the right circumstance and with the right execution.

THE SITUATION:
Your 18-year-old son just gets word that he has been rejected by his top college choice. You are on your way home from work and you can sense the mood in the house is quite somber. Your son is putting up a brave face, but you can hear it in his voice the disappointment is deep.

THE PLAY (SERVANT)

You talk to your wife on the phone and decide it is time for a surprise onside kick. It is time to celebrate you son for who he is, forget the idiot elite colleges that do not know better! You make arrangements to bring home his favorite food and dessert and you invite his closest buddy over to partake. You also order three tickets to the latest action movie for you, your son and his buddy to go to that night. So what if the movie starts at 10:00 pm and ends at midnight—you are going for it.

COACH PAT'S PLAYBOOK

"The moments of happiness we enjoy take us by surprise. It is not that we seize them, but that they seize us."

— Ashley Montagu

PENALTY FLAG: DON'T BE THAT GUY (TALKER)...

The father who pulls off the surprise and then makes the rest of the evening about how great a father he is. This is a night to celebrate your son. If you stay low-key and sincere, your son will remember this night.

WRISTBAND

The Play = Servant, the spontaneous father
Penalty = Talker, the selfish father

PLAY #27

Hard Count

DEFINITION:
The quarterback is trying to draw the opposing defensive linemen offsides by using a cadence where certain sounds are louder (hut, hut, HUT).

OLD SCHOOL: *Dan Fouts*, San Diego Chargers
MODERN: *Peyton Manning*, Indianapolis Colts/Denver Broncos

THE SKINNY:
The best way to avoid getting beat by the hard count is to simulate it in practice. Stressful situations are made easier when our kids have seen them before.

THE SITUATION:
Your 12-year-old daughter got a poor grade on an English paper and is quite upset. She worked hard on the paper and the teacher did not provide much reasoning for the poor grade. The teacher is a veteran male teacher who knows his stuff, but can be gruff and intimidating to students. Your daughter does not feel comfortable talking to him.

THE PLAY (PRO)

You sit down with your daughter and talk about the paper. It is clear to both you and her that she needs to go and talk to the teacher. She is scared to talk with the teacher and worried that he will be sarcastic and belittling. You talk through her fears with her and ask, "What is the worst thing that could happen?" When she talks about being embarrassed, reassure her that her interaction with the teacher will never change the way you feel about her. Next, you spring into role-play mode. You are the gruff English teacher and she is coming to talk to you. Get into the role and ask tough questions to your daughter. At a natural stopping point, review the interaction and then try it again. Three or four practice sessions will give your daughter the confidence to succeed.

COACH PAT'S PLAYBOOK

Never run an important play in a game that you have not practiced.

PENALTY FLAG: DON'T BE THAT GUY (TALKER)...

The father who puts on his Superman cape and rescues his daughter by talking to the English teacher himself. Give your daughter the tools to talk with the teacher and if that does not work, then it is time to talk to the teacher yourself.

WRISTBAND

The Play = Pro, the rehearsing father
Penalty = Talker, the rescuing father

PLAY #28
Overtime

DEFINITION:
The game is tied at the end of regulation time and an extra session is needed to determine a winner.

OLD SCHOOL: Miami Dolphins vs Kansas City Chiefs, 1971
MODERN: New England Patriots vs Oakland Raiders (tuck rule), 2001

THE SKINNY:
Staying up late and putting in a little extra time can make all the difference.

THE SITUATION:
Your 16-year-old daughter is at a sleepover, and at 11 p.m., you receive an urgent text that she wants to be picked up and come home. You pick her up and she is obviously upset about the dynamics with her friends. She explains that she feels like an outsider who doesn't fit in anywhere. She is trying to be brave, but her voice is starting to quiver.

THE PLAY (GURU)

As you walk towards the house, you suggest that the two of you head to the family room to discuss things further. This discussion could last anywhere from 10 minutes to two hours. If the discussion is shorter, suggest that the two of you make popcorn and watch a favorite move afterwards. If the discussion is longer, simply focus on hearing your daughter out. Make sure you tell your daughter how great she is and reinforce it with a hug. Your evening will not probably end until after 2 a.m., but the impact will be worth it.

COACH PAT'S PLAYBOOK

In moments of identity crisis, teenagers simply want to know that they are important and loved.

PENALTY FLAG: DON'T BE THAT GUY (WIMP)...

The father who says he is too tired to stay up because he has an early golf game the next morning. This father has not so subtly told his daughter where his real priorities are located.

WRISTBAND

The Play = Guru, the wise father
Penalty = Wimp, the weak father

PLAY #29
Two Minute Drill

DEFINITION:
The offense plays in hurry-up mode and typically goes without a huddle in order to score quickly at the end of a half, or end of the game.

OLD SCHOOL: *Joe Montana* leads 49ers on game-winning drive in Super Bowl XXIII
MODERN: *Ben Roethlisberger* leads Steelers on game-winning drive in Super Bowl XLIII

THE SKINNY:
Speed, focus and discipline are needed to make important deadlines.

THE SITUATION:
Your 16-year-old son has a large English paper due in a week and he has barely started reading the book associated with the paper. You are extremely frustrated with his continued procrastination, but you also know that this paper will go a long way toward determining his grade.

THE PLAY (PRO)

Sit down with your son and briefly express that you are disappointed that he is caught in this predicament with his paper. Tell him that you and he will discuss the larger issue of procrastination after the paper is completed. Right now it is time to go into action mode. Start by working backwards from when the paper is due. The paper is due on a Friday, so the final editing must be done by Thursday, the rough draft by Wednesday, the paper outline by Monday and the book must be read by Sunday. It is currently Saturday and he has 180 pages left to read. Simple: he needs to read 90 pages on both Saturday and Sunday. All other activities become secondary for the week, including sports, if they interfere with this schedule.

COACH PAT'S PLAYBOOK

In Stephen Covey's *7 Habits of Highly Effective People*, Habit #2 is *Begin with the End in Mind*. This habit challenges us to take a step back, create the success blueprint we want in our head, then execute the plan.

PENALTY FLAG: DON'T BE THAT GUY (SERVANT)...

The father who panics and basically writes the paper for his son. Remember, your son's life does not end at age 16. There are larger life lessons at stake here.

WRISTBAND

The Play = Pro, the balanced father
Penalty = Servant, the overly invested father

PLAY #30

The Zone Blitz

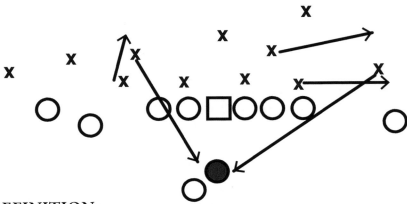

DEFINITION:

The defense applies pressure by blitzing from unexpected places and will even drop defensive linemen into coverage.

OLD SCHOOL: Pittsburgh Steelers under defensive coordinator *Dick Lebeau* (1990's)

MODERN: Baltimore Ravens under defensive coordinator *Rex Ryan* (2000's)

THE SKINNY:

Getting involved in an unexpected area can pay major dividends.

THE SITUATION:

Your 14-year daughter is struggling in her first year of high school, especially in her math class. Historically, your spouse has been the person to deal directly with the school on academic issues. You have been supportive, but always a secondary player.

THE PLAY (PRO)

Tell your wife that you would like to be directly involved with the math teacher. Email the teacher and set up a time to talk either in person or on the phone. Ask the teacher what your daughter's #1 issue is in the class and what can be done at home to support her. Armed with the information, set up a time to talk with your daughter and your wife about the math class. Take the lead in the discussion and be positive and supportive, but let your daughter know that you expect different results.

COACH PAT'S PLAYBOOK

When a father takes a family issue seriously, it typically becomes an important issue for the entire family.

PENALTY FLAG: DON'T BE THAT GUY (WIMP)...

The father who, after to going to one academic meeting, now becomes an expert on all things pertaining to school and need to be given credit.

WRISTBAND

The Play = Pro, the responsible father
Penalty = Wimp, the needy father

PLAY #31

Squib Kick

DEFINITION:
The team kicking off plays it safe by kicking away from a dangerous return man on the other team.

OLD SCHOOL: Kicking away from *Desmond Howard*, Green Bay Packers
MODERN: Kicking away from *Devin Hester*, Chicago Bears

THE SKINNY:
Sometimes playing it safe to prevent a larger problem is a good move.

THE SITUATION:
Your 13-year old son has been hanging with a new group of friends, including some girls that you are not totally comfortable with. You do not know the parents of these kids and just are not sure of the healthiness of these relationships. On the other hand, your son, who has struggled with friendships, appears to be happier than he has been in a long time.

THE PLAY (PRO)

Tell your son that you would be happy to have his friends over to your house and even volunteer to pick them up. You will learn a ton about his friends just by listening in the car and seeing them interact around your house. Withhold any judgments, simply be an observer of the situation.

COACH PAT'S PLAYBOOK

The car is the #1 place to talk to your teenager, but also to gain insight into your teen's friends and activities. The car is the perfect combination of having a captive audience and just enough distraction to facilitate discussion.

PENALTY FLAG: DON'T BE THAT GUY (VOLCANO)...

The father who invites his son's friends over, but secretly resents it and is uptight the entire time the kids are at his house. This father keeps interrupting the activities of his son and friends with phony excuses for coming into the basement.

WRISTBAND
The Play = Pro, the involved father
Penalty = Volcano, the resentful father

PLAY #32

Cover Zero

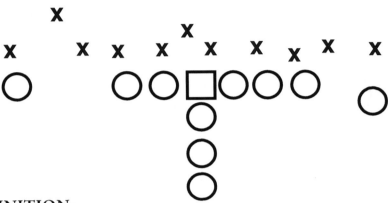

DEFINITION:

The defense aligns in an aggressive formation, where there is not a safety back deep to provide ultimate protection.

OLD SCHOOL: Chicago Bears "46" defense
MODERN: Pittsburgh Steelers 2000s

THE SKINNY:

Sometimes removing all backup coverage and letting our children endure natural consequences is the best move to make.

THE SITUATION:

Your 15-year-old daughter has been procrastinating on getting her service hours done for her civics class. You have talked with her repeatedly, set up schedules, begged and cajoled her and nothing has seemed to work. It is becoming increasingly apparent to you that she will not complete her hours and thus not get credit for the course.

THE PLAY (GURU)

After weeks or even months of monitoring and helping, it is time to back off and let the natural consequences run their course. Tell your daughter that you will let her handle the service hours. When your daughter is in a panic on the last weekend when she clearly will not have enough hours, you can show you care, but do not rush in to save her. Let her endure the natural consequences of not getting credit for the course or having to repeat the service hours in the summer. There will definitely by short-term pain, but the long-term gain is worth it.

COACH PAT'S PLAYBOOK

Washing machines get clothes clean through agitation. Sometime the status quo needs to be upset for larger change to happen.

PENALTY FLAG: DON'T BE THAT GUY (VOLCANO)...

The father who gleefully tells his daughter, "I warned you." or "I told you so." Shaming is never a great strategy, but even less so when people are in crisis.

WRISTBAND

The Play = Guru, the thoughtful father
Penalty = Volcano, the spiteful father

PLAY #33
Double Coverage

X   X   X
X   X X   X   X   X   X   X
O   O O □ O O O   O

          O
          O
          O

DEFINITION:
A wide receiver is covered by two defenders, typically a cornerback and a safety over the top.

OLD SCHOOL: *Lynn Swann*, Pittsburgh Steelers
MODERN: *Larry Fitzgerald*, Arizona Cardinals

THE SKINNY:
On big issues, it is critical that the two parents stay on the same page. If there is only one parent, then bringing in another adult is helpful.

THE SITUATION:
Your 16-year-old son has broken his curfew for the third time. He was only 15 minutes late this time, but there is a clear pattern of not paying enough attention to time. Next weekend there is a large community event that he is asking to attend. You and your spouse are debating whether to let him go to the event.

THE PLAY (PRO)

You and your spouse need to have a pre-meeting before you talk with your son. In that meeting, hash out all the arguments on both sides and come to an agreement that you can both support. When you talk to your son, it is critical that you are both there and that you present a united front. Use the language of "we" and "our" when you are talking about the decision and make sure both people talk.

COACH PAT'S PLAYBOOK

Children are absolute masters at spotting weakness and indecision. If they sense any division between you and your spouse, they will exploit it.

PENALTY FLAG: DON'T BE THAT GUY (VOLCANO)...

The father who throws his spouse under the bus, by saying, "I really wanted to let you go, but your mother was against it." These types of statements make you look weak and damage your credibility with both your spouse and son.

WRISTBAND

The Play = Pro, the teammate father
Penalty = Volcano, the rogue father

PLAY #34
2-Point Conversion

DEFINITION:
After a touchdown is scored the offense elects to go for a higher risk, higher reward play that could result in two points, rather than the extra point.

OLD SCHOOL: Boise State over Oklahoma (Fiesta Bowl 2007)
MODERN: Oregon Ducks

THE SKINNY:
The two-point conversion is almost always executed when a team is trailing and desperate to get back into the game.

THE SITUATION:
Your 13-year-old daughter is barely speaking to you after the latest incident where she claims you embarrassed her in front of her friends. You thought you were just joking around, but her teary-eyed response of "Just stay away from me and my friends!" was absolutely no joke. You are not sure how to repair the damage.

THE PLAY (PRO)

The high-risk call is to ask to meet with your daughter privately, apologize for embarrassing her and then present her with a letter that explains how you really feel about her. The letter should be short, direct and heartfelt. It is imperative that you take full responsibility for your actions in the letter and not try to justify yourself. This is the type of letter that could fundamentally shift how you relate to your daughter.

COACH PAT'S PLAYBOOK

Not all moments in life are equal. Some moments matter more than others. When relationships are at a tipping point, our actions in those moments are critical.

PENALTY FLAG: DON'T BE THAT GUY (WIMP)...

The father who tries to minimize and invalidate his daughter's pain by saying he did not mean to upset her. This father tries to undo a bad joke by making more jokes.

WRISTBAND

The Play = Pro, the risk-taking father
Penalty = Wimp, the invalidating father

PLAY #35

Mike Blitz

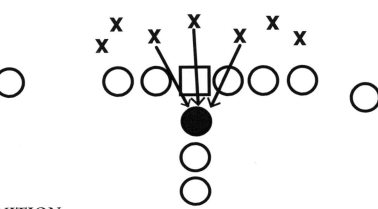

DEFINITION:
The middle linebacker blitzes right up the middle and tries to tackle either the ballcarrier or the quarterback.

OLD SCHOOL: *Dick Butkus*, Chicago Bears
MODERN: *Ray Lewis*, Baltimore Ravens

THE SKINNY:
Charging directly at your target can sometimes be the best move.

THE SITUATION:
Your 15-year-old son was suspended from school for getting into a fight with another student.

THE PLAY (PRO)

No sense in playing around: get right to the facts. Ask your son the Who, What, Where, When and Why of the fight situation. Listen intently in a nonjudgmental manner and ask follow up questions where appropriate. Sort out the chronology of the events and the feelings as they developed. Helping your son understand the triggers for his behavior and his own emotions is critical to him using this incident as a learning experience.

COACH PAT'S PLAYBOOK

Elephants in the room and unanswered questions don't help anyone. Being bold and willing to ask tough questions will save a lot of headaches later.

PENALTY FLAG: DON'T BE THAT GUY (VOLCANO)...

The father who reads his son the Riot Act and does not give him a chance to explain his side of the story. It is important to listen attentively and establish the facts of the incident before responding.

WRISTBAND

The Play = Pro, the thorough father
Penalty = Volcano, the irrational father

PLAY #36

Timeout

DEFINITION:
Called by the head coach to either save time or change the momentum at a key moment in the game.

OLD SCHOOL: *Hank Stram*, Kansas City Chiefs
MODERN: *Bill Cowher*, Pittsburgh Steelers

THE SKINNY:
Key moments in life call for taking a step back and having a discussion.

THE SITUATION:
Your 17-year-old daughter has been asked to the prom by a very high profile senior in the school. She is excited, but nervous about the group she will be going with because they are known as a party crew. You do not want to put a damper on your daughter's prom, but you are concerned that she could be headed into uncharted territory with drug, alcohol and sexual issues.

THE PLAY (PRO)

A few nights before the prom, sit down with your daughter and walk through the entire prom timeline from pictures to final drop-off. Talk candidly about alcohol, drugs and sexual activity and what to do to avoid uncomfortable situations. Tell her that you are only a phone call or text away and that you are willing to pick her up at any time in the evening if things are uncomfortable.

COACH PAT'S PLAYBOOK

Consistently communicating that we are interested in our children's safety is key. Let them know that their physical and emotional well-being is your greatest concern.

PENALTY FLAG: DON'T BE THAT GUY (WIMP)...

The father who ignores his daughter's concerns and tells her to just have fun. Ignoring potential red flags does not make them go away.

WRISTBAND

The Play = Pro, the candid father
Penalty = Wimp, the denial father

END OF THIRD QUARTER

Sideline Reporter

THE DATE WAS SEPTEMBER 5, 1983. The location: Fargo, ND. My American Legion baseball team, Edina Post 471, was playing for the National Championship against the defending national champs, Boyertown, PA. It was the 9th inning and we trailed 4-3 with two outs and a runner on first base. Our lead-off hitter Carl Ramseth was tenaciously fouling off pitches to save our season. I waited nervously in the on-deck circle, wondering if I would get a chance to bat. On the seventh pitch, Carl lofted a short flyball to left field. I lowered my head and thought, *2nd place in the country isn't so bad.*

As I looked up, I saw Boyertown's shortstop Greg Gilbert frantically sprinting towards the outfield as the leftfielder came charging in. Then, wham!!! Gilbert and the leftfielder collided in a football-like collision and the ball trickled out towards the foul line. Paul Kemble, our runner on first, raced all the way around to score, Carl ended up on 2nd base and there was pandemonium throughout the 3,500 faithful fans. Our bench was going absolutely ballistic, and all I could think was: I am up now.

But the problem was that I wasn't really up quite yet. The collision was so severe that the Boyertown left fielder had to be taken to the hospital. For 45 long minutes, I waited to bat in the 9th inning of a tied national championship game.

A funny thing happened along the way to me getting nervous and psyching myself out before the at-bat. I looked in the stands and saw my dad. He looked right back at me and gave me a confident nod that intimated, "You're the man, go up and get this thing done." My mind was flooded with all the memories of playing and practicing baseball for years with my dad. My dad had coached me from

Little League all the way to age sixteen. Long-ago batting practice and fielding practice sessions from Normandale and Braemar Park danced in my mind's eye. Going for ice cream after games and drinking A & W root beer with my dad flashed before me. And then I became totally calm. No nerves. No worrying about being a hero or goat, just thoughts of, "see the ball, hit the ball," just like my dad taught me.

I am happy to report that on the fourth pitch I ripped a single to right field to give us a 5-4 lead, and we held on in the bottom of the inning to claim the National Championship. Being one of the heroes was great, but the moment I locked gazes with my dad is a precious memory for the rest of my life.

FOURTH QUARTER

*Unique Formations,
Personal Dominance
& Trick Plays*

PLAY #37
Unbalanced Line Run

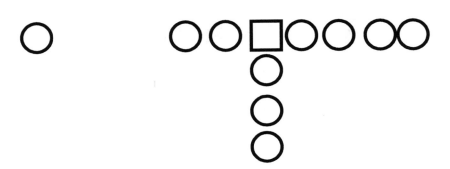

DEFINITION:
The unbalanced line puts an extra offensive lineman on one side of the ball and typically teams will run that direction.

OLD SCHOOL: Nebraska Cornhuskers
MODERN: LSU Tigers

THE SKINNY:
Sometimes resources cannot be equally divided amongst your children. In certain situations, going "unbalanced" on one child is the best move to make.

THE SITUATION:
Your 12-year-old son is struggling with the transition to middle school. He is disorganized, losing things and getting below average grades in school. His frustration level has reached a boiling point by the 3rd week of school. The entire family is being disrupted by the stress created by your middle school son.

THE PLAY (SERVANT)

Time to sit down with your son, help him clean out his backpack and then make a daily plan for success. This will include helping him create a system to record his "to-dos" and to organize all his papers and assignments. In the beginning, it will probably take an hour to create the system and then 15-20 minute meetings nightly for the next three weeks until the new system becomes a habit. Patience, consistency and positive reinforcement are the key to making this play work.

COACH PAT'S PLAYBOOK

The transition to multiple teachers in middle school is often a rough transition for boys. All the papers that used to be kept in a single desk drawer are now in multiple folders and a locker. This is probably the first time that an organizational system is important for his success.

PENALTY FLAG: DON'T BE THAT GUY (TALKER)...

The father who talks about how disorganized he was in school. This intuitively sends the message that it is okay to be disorganized, because look at dad, he is successful. Also, be careful about comparing your disorganized child to your child who is perfectly organized.

WRISTBAND

The Play = Servant, the patient father
Penalty = Talker, the rationalizing father

PLAY #38

Triple Option

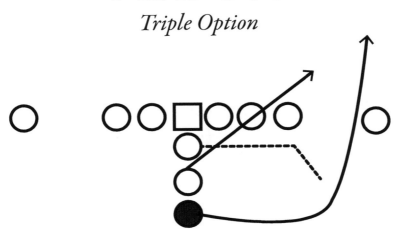

DEFINITION:
The quarterback takes the snap from center and has the option of handing the ball off, pitching the ball or keeping it himself.

OLD SCHOOL: Oklahoma Sooners 1970s
MODERN: Army Cadets & Navy Midshipmen 2000s

THE SKINNY:
Choices or options in life create motivation for everyone, including our children. Choice, rather than prescription, is the best way to get things done.

THE SITUATION:
Your 16-year-old daughter has gotten into the routine of Facebooking, texting, reading novels and lying around the house during the summer. You would like her to contribute more to the well-being of the household or earn some money outside of the house.

THE PLAY (GURU)

Approach your daughter when both of you are feeling good, maybe right after a meal. Talk to her by yourself (or with your spouse) and lay out your thoughts on her being more active and involved during the summer. Give her three options to think about: 1) Complete a daily list of agreed-upon chores. 2) Pursue babysitting during the day. 3) Get a job at a local restaurant or shop. Give her 24 hours to think about the options and then have a second conversation to establish a game plan.

COACH PAT'S PLAYBOOK

Researcher Daniel Pink says there are three things that motivate in the 21st century: Autonomy (choice), Mastery (competence) and Meaning (purpose).

– Daniel Pink, *The Drive*

PENALTY FLAG: DON'T BE THAT GUY (TALKER)...

The father who verbally sideswipes his daughter while she is reading and asks her when she is going to get a job or start cleaning the house. For good measure, this father pours on a guilt trip by mentioning how hard he and her mother work.

WRISTBAND

The Play = Guru, the big picture father
Penalty = Volcano, the stealth bomber father

PLAY #39

Pistol Formation

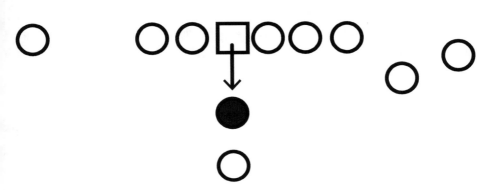

DEFINITION:
The quarterback takes the snap 2-3 yards behind the line of scrimmage, in between a traditional under center approach and a deeper shotgun approach.

OLD SCHOOL: *Chris Ault*, Nevada (coach)
MODERN: *Colin Kaepernick*, San Francisco 49ers

THE SKINNY:
Sometimes a new approach (formation) is helpful to solve an old problem.

THE SITUATION:
You and your twelve-year old daughter have an icy relationship. You communicate only when necessary and there is an air of tension whenever the two of you are in the same room. She discloses only totally necessary information to you. You would like to see your relationship go to another more positive level.

THE PLAY (PRO)

Since the old plays are not working, time to go to a totally new approach. Tell your daughter you would like to meet with her about something important when she has some free time. Get in a comfortable, private setting and tell her that you are bummed that you and her do not have a better relationship. Take responsibility for the mistakes you have made and ask her how she thinks the relationship can get better. Be careful about going too much into her negative behavior, but it is okay to talk about your own feelings of hurt and disappointment. End the meeting by setting up another time to talk, perhaps with food involved.

COACH PAT'S PLAYBOOK

When trust has been broken in a relationship, most people react by either becoming angry or going into victim mode. We have to be willing to stay with people while they are in the victim and anger stages, until they are ready to engage at a higher level.

PENALTY FLAG: DON'T BE THAT GUY (VOLCANO)...

The father who baits and switches his daughter by launching into a tirade about her behavior during the meeting. The trust is already fragile in this relationship, it is important that this initial meeting does not contain any major surprises.

WRISTBAND

The Play = Pro, the flexible father
Penalty = Volcano, the deceptive father

PLAY #40

Pancake Block

DEFINITION:
An offensive lineman not only defeats his man, he knocks him on his back and typically falls on him.

OLD SCHOOL: *Anthony Munoz*, Cincinnati Bengals
MODERN: *Jonathan Ogden*, Baltimore

THE SKINNY:
Sometimes standing up for our kids in a crisis with total focus and force is what is necessary.

THE SITUATION:
Your thirteen-year old son is being bullied by a couple of 14-year-old boys. You have advised your son to stand up for himself and you have even had a chat with the bully's father. Nothing has seemed to work and the problem has in fact gotten worse, with a bad incident this past weekend.

THE PLAY (PRO)

Time for a little more direct action. You leave work early and go to where you know the bully hangs out after school. You politely introduce yourself and then explain the distress your son has felt. You are certain that the bully does not want to cause this type of problem and that the behavior will stop. You will assume that the behavior will stop, if it does not, then you will be forced to go the more formal route of reporting the behavior to authorities. Explain that you do not want to do that and would rather have the issued solved right now.

COACH PAT'S PLAYBOOK

Bullying behavior is about control and power. Most bullies have been bullied themselves, so their bullying behavior is a way to gain some power back.

PENALTY FLAG: DON'T BE THAT GUY (VOLCANO)...

The father who comes in guns blazing and threatens the bully. This will not solve the bullying problem and will exasperate your relationship with your son.

WRISTBAND

The Play = Pro, the courageous father
Penalty = Volcano, the bullying father

PLAY #41

Stiff Arm

DEFINITION:
The running back extends his arm into the chest or shoulder of a would-be tackler in order to reject the tackler and avoid being taken down.

OLD SCHOOL: *Jim Brown*, Cleveland Browns
MODERN: *Walter Payton*, Chicago Bears

THE SKINNY:
Rejecting a certain behavior or situation is sometimes the best course of action.

THE SITUATION:
Your 14-year-old daughter has become interested in an 18-year-old boy. He does not appear to be a malicious kid, but you wonder why he is trying to date your freshman daughter, when he is a senior. Your daughter is inexperienced with relationships and appears to have really fallen hard for this senior.

THE PLAY (PRO)

Before they are officially dating, you and your spouse sit down and talk to your daughter about your concerns. Express directly that you are uncomfortable with her dating a boy that much older and you do not support it. Your daughter might be relieved with the boundary you have put up for her, but more than likely she will be hurt by your lack of trust in her judgment. Explain to her that when matters of safety are involved, there is very little room to negotiate. It is important to keep the dialogue going and be willing to adjust your stance as new information becomes available.

COACH PAT'S PLAYBOOK

When safety is the paramount concern, then teen input and parental flexibility are much less important.

PENALTY FLAG: DON'T BE THAT GUY (VOLCANO)...

The father who shows no empathy for his daughter as he tells her she cannot date the 18-year-old boy. Love, no matter how silly or unrealistic, creates powerful emotions that should not be shut down or trivialized.

WRISTBAND
The Play = Pro, the direct father
Penalty = Volcano, the insensitive father

PLAY #42

Flea Flicker

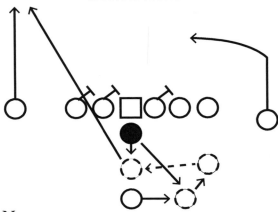

DEFINITION:
Quarterback hands the ball to the running back who pretends to run and then pitches the ball back to the quarterback who throws a long pass.

OLD SCHOOL: *Phil Simms* to *Joe Morris* to *Phil McConkey* SB XXI
MODERN: *Kurt Warner* to *JJ Arrington* to *Larry Fitzgerald*, NFC Championship 2009

THE SKINNY:
A little deception can lead to a big result.

THE SITUATION:
Your 16-year-old son has his first soccer game of the season, but you have a critical, late-afternoon meeting, so you have told him that you will miss the game. He is disappointed, but understands that you will not be in attendance.

THE PLAY (PRO)

You work quietly behind the scenes to either get the meeting time changed, get someone to replace you or participate in the meeting via technology. Once you have the details arranged, do not say anything to your son. Just show up at the game and stand near the edge of the bleachers so he can see you. When you make eye contact, give him a thumbs up and tell him to have a great game.

COACH PAT'S PLAYBOOK

Surprise is not just an element for younger children. An unexpected positive surprise creates an emotional bond and strengthens your overall relationship.

PENALTY FLAG: DON'T BE THAT GUY (TALKER)...

The father who makes it to the game and then does not really watch the game, but instead spends his time checking emails. Be present in both body and spirit.

WRISTBAND

The Play = Pro, the prioritizing father
Penalty = Talker, the inattentive father

PLAY #43
Quick Count

DEFINITION:
The quarterback comes to the line of scrimmage and the ball is snapped quickly with the idea of surprising the defense.

OLD SCHOOL: *Fran Tarkenton*, Minnesota Vikings
MODERN: *John Elway*, Denver Broncos

THE SKINNY:
A quick response to an issue can keep things from escalating.

THE SITUATION:
You and your 18-year-old daughter just finished an unpleasant discussion where you were talking about her work around the house. In frustration, you lost your temper during the discussion. You have to run to a board meeting, so there are lingering bad feelings as you drive away. There is not a crisis with your daughter, but you don't feel good about how things ended.

THE PLAY (PRO)

Send your daughter a quick text from your meeting and apologize for losing your temper. On your way home from the meeting, make a quick stop at the gas station and purchase a card, flowers or a favorite snack for her. If she is still awake, go into her room and present the gift and finish the conversation. If she is not awake, place the gift with an appropriate note next to her bed.

COACH PAT'S PLAYBOOK

Admitting mistakes and being willing to apologize communicates humility, self-awareness and respect to our children.

PENALTY FLAG: DON'T BE THAT GUY (WIMP)...

The father who sort-of apologizes, but then justifies himself by making some excuses. If you are going to apologize, then just do it! Do not add any unnecessary qualifiers.

WRISTBAND
The Play = Pro, the thoughtful father
Penalty = Wimp, the "yeah, but" father

PLAY #44
QB Draw

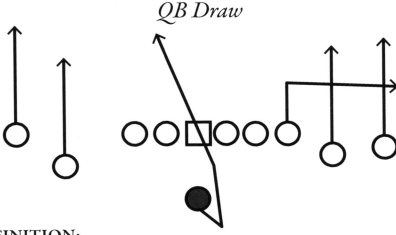

DEFINITION:
The quarterback drops back like he is going to pass and then tucks the ball and finds a running lane.

OLD SCHOOL: *Steve Young*, San Francisco 49ers
MODERN: *Russell Wilson*, Seattle Seahawks

THE SKINNY:
Taking matters into your own hands can be the way to solve problems.

THE SITUATION:
Your 2nd grade son is struggling in school. Last year he loved school, but now he constantly complains about stomach aches and begs to not attend school. You know that his teacher is a little bit of an "old school yeller" and you think that has affected your son.

THE PLAY (GURU)

Set up a parental conference with the teacher immediately to get her input on the situation. Listen carefully to what she says is happening with your son. As the conversation evolves, do not hesitate to mention that your son is more motivated by encouragement than by direct confrontation. Give her a chance to explain herself.

COACH PAT'S PLAYBOOK

When the power dynamic is heavily weighed against your kids, it is time to level the playing field by becoming directly involved.

PENALTY FLAG: DON'T BE THAT GUY (WIMP)...

The father who is too busy to ever come home early to take care of the problem. Work issues are certainly important, but your child's success in school ranks right up there in importance.

WRISTBAND

The Play = Guru, the patient father
Penalty = Wimp, the disengaged father

PLAY #45
Hook & Ladder

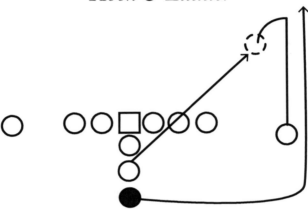

DEFINITION:
A trick play where the wide receiver runs a simple hook pattern, catches the ball and then laterals to another player running by.

OLD SCHOOL: *Isaac Curtis*, Cincinnati Bengals
MODERN: Boise State vs Oklahoma, Fiesta Bowl 2007

THE SKINNY:
A regular event can be made special by adding something unexpected.

THE SITUATION:
Your 17-year-old daughter has earned excellent grades during the first semester of her junior year. The family is going to celebrate with a dinner at her favorite restaurant.

THE PLAY (PRO)

At dinner, you pull out a gift certificate to your daughter's favorite store and present it to her. After dinner you suggest getting ice cream and eating it at home. While at the ice cream shop, you text her three closest friends with a pre-arranged signal to show up on your front porch in fifteen minutes. As your car pulls up to the house, your daughter will be smiling as she sees her best friends on the front porch.

COACH PAT'S PLAYBOOK

The amount of planning put into an event is usually directly correlated with the emotional impact of the event. When we put in extra time, we are simply saying to another person, "You are important."

PENALTY FLAG: DON'T BE THAT GUY (TALKER)...

The father who cannot keep a secret and tells his daughter about the friends coming over for ice cream. The power in this event is in the element of surprise.

WRISTBAND

The Play = Pro, the planning father
Penalty = Talker, the immature father

PLAY #46

Double Move

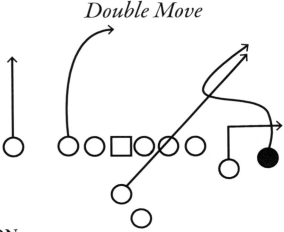

DEFINITION:
The receiver fakes going one direction and then goes another as in a post-corner route.

OLD SCHOOL: *Michael Irvin*, Dallas Cowboys
MODERN: *Anquan Bolden*, Baltimore Ravens

THE SKINNY:
Things are not always as they appear. We need to be able to confront a double life.

THE SITUATION:
Your 17-year-old son has always been an easy kid to raise. He has done well in school, participated in sports and been helpful around the house. Lately, you have seen a big change in attitude as he has joined a new group of friends. He has been disrespectful, evasive and has unaccounted for time that you worry about. His jacket recently reeked of smoke, which he claims came from one of his friends. He is not engaged at home and seems quite secretive. You are worried that there is a larger problem going on.

THE PLAY (PRO)

You need to gently, but firmly confront your son with the changes you see. Ask him if everything is okay. Also, communicate that deception and dishonesty is one of the worst things for a relationship. Tell him you would rather hear bad news in an honest manner than to be deceived. You will most likely receive a defensive response or no response, but this sets the table for future discussions. You want to communicate love, but also communicate that you know what is going on.

COACH PAT'S PLAYBOOK

When small acts of deception are not confronted, we are setting the table for real trouble. Confront the small and the large thing will not happen.

PENALTY FLAG: DON'T BE THAT GUY (WIMP)...

The father who ignores small patterns of deception and hopes they will go away. Most large deceptions start as a series of smaller lies.

WRISTBAND

The Play = Pro, the balanced father
Penalty = Wimp, the denial father

PLAY #47
The Hail Mary

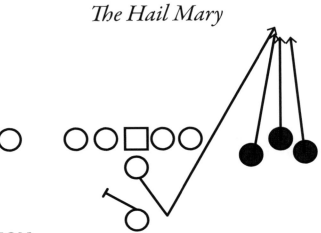

DEFINITION:
The offense throws a desperation long pass into a crowd at the end of a game, hoping to somehow get lucky and score a touchdown.

OLD SCHOOL: *Roger Staubach* to *Drew Pearson* for the Cowboys over the Vikings 1975 NFC Playoffs
MODERN: *Doug Flutie* (Boston College) to *Gerard Phelan* over the Miami Hurricanes 1984

THE SKINNY:
Desperate times sometimes call for desperate measures.

THE SITUATION:
Your 18-year old daughter is a college freshman at a university that is three hours from your house. She is having a hard time adjusting and really misses her family and friends, three months into the school year. You talk to her via Skype on a Saturday and can hear the sadness in her voice. She seems depressed and lethargic.

THE PLAY (SERVANT)

You suggest to your wife that the two of you drive down and visit your daughter on Sunday. You go out and pick up some of her favorite food and a gift certificate to a favorite restaurant that she can use at college. You text your daughter on Saturday night and say you will be on campus to take her to lunch on Sunday. You leave early on Sunday morning, hang out with your daughter until about 5 p.m. and then return to your house. A long, tiring day, but truly worth it.

COACH PAT'S PLAYBOOK

Never underestimate the impact of a large gesture. When we put extraordinary effort in, it connects to the emotions and heart of another person.

PENALTY FLAG: DON'T BE THAT GUY (WIMP)...

The father who makes excuses about having to complete some work tasks or says it is too long of drive for one day. There will always be reasons not to do extraordinary things.

WRISTBAND
The Play = Servant, the sacrificing father
Penalty = Wimp, the excuse-making father

PLAY #48
Victory Formation

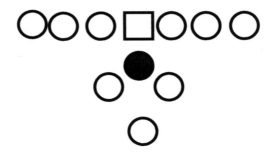

DEFINITION:
Play that is typically done at the end of a game when victory is assured and all that is left is for the quarterback to kneel down and run out the clock.

OLD SCHOOL: *Herm Edwards* scoring on Miracle in the Meadowland 1978
MODERN: *Phillip Rivers* fumbling vs KC Chiefs 2011

THE SKINNY:
It is important to celebrate "wins" in life whenever they occur.

THE SITUATION:
Your 11-year old son has battled all year in a rugged math class. The teacher has not been really helpful, so your son has developed alternative ways to learn the material, including organizing study groups, Facebook chats and going to other teachers. Your son finished the course by getting a "B" on his report card, his highest grade for the year.

THE PLAY (PRO)

Take your son out for a special lunch or dinner at his favorite hangout place. Tell him how much you appreciate his hard work and perseverance this year in math class. Connect his hard work and effort to the type of traits that help make people successful for the long term. Emphasize to your son that life is about growth and improvement.

COACH PAT'S PLAYBOOK

Researcher Angela Duckworth has identified "grit" as the key variable for success in any large endeavor. Grit is the ability to stick with long-term goals, persist and effectively deal with disappointment and setbacks.

PENALTY FLAG: DON'T BE THAT GUY (VOLCANO)...

The father who congratulates his son on getting a "B" and then immediately mentions how he got an "A" in math class. This is invalidating and deflating for your son.

WRISTBAND

The Play = Pro, the celebratory father
Penalty = Volcano, the comparing father

END OF
GAME
INTERVIEW

GREAT FATHERS, LIKE GREAT FOOTBALL PLAYERS, ARE PLAYMAKERS. They are fearless men who are not satisfied with just being good enough. The great father wants to excel and to make a difference in his kids' lives and the lives of others. Great fathers are not perfect, but they are growth-oriented. Day after day, the great ones are picking up new skills, ideas and plays. Great fathers read books and blogs ask tons of questions and are willing to get out of their comfort zone. These men understand that fathering is a high calling, where the stakes are high and the potential rewards are huge.

Most of all, great fathers value their children. Whether with their newborn daughter or with their 18-year-old son, the great ones are totally present. Their children feel like they are the only thing in the world that matters and that is where the true magic of fatherhood happens.

So, go out and make plays! Be bold and daring and caring and awesome. Let the great father within you out to roam the field of life and truly make a difference.

POST-GAME INFORMATION

About the Author

PATRICK DONOHUE is a former Division I athlete and athletic coach. He has spent the last twenty-two years as a teacher, administrator and coach in a high school setting. Today, his company Donohue Consulting Inc. (www.donohuelifecoaching.com) specializes in providing coaching and leadership training for corporate and educational professionals.

Patrick is a licensed professional coach (ACC) who works with clients that range from corporate and educational leaders to students. He is certified as a Stakeholder Centered Coach (Marshall Goldsmith Institute) and is a certified as an Energy Leadership Index Master Practitioner. He has led leadership trainings in the Health Care and Educational industries. Patrick speaks extensively on topics such as Developing Grit, The Leader as Coach and Forming Championship Teams. He writes a blog for men who want to be great fathers called AlignMENt. He is passionate about the critical role that men play in the development of their children.

Patrick lives in Oak Park, IL with his wife Binita and their two children, Sarina and Shaan. You can contact him at patrick@donohuelifecoaching.com.